Original title:
The Secret Life of Soil

Copyright © 2025 Creative Arts Management OÜ
All rights reserved.

Author: George Mercer
ISBN HARDBACK: 978-1-80581-777-2
ISBN PAPERBACK: 978-1-80581-304-0
ISBN EBOOK: 978-1-80581-777-2

A Beneath-The-Soil Reverie

In the dark, the roots all dance,
Among the critters, they take a chance.
Rabbits nibble on a leafy treat,
While ants march off on tiny feet.

Wiggly worms wear party hats,
Mixing soil while avoiding chats.
A mole pops up to join the fun,
Declare a feast when day is done.

The Unseen Network of Nutrients

Beneath the grass, a network glows,
With whispers shared among the rows.
Carrots gossip with peas so sweet,
Planning mischief with every beet.

Radishes grumble, "We've got style!"
While potatoes boast with a cheeky smile.
In this realm, there's no dispute,
They're all just rooting for a cute shoot.

Echoes from the Earth's Heart

Beneath the ground, the rhymes unfold,
Tiny dialogues of earth so bold.
The rocks and seeds, they hum along,
Creating melodies like a song.

Mice tap dance to rhythmic sways,
While fungi join and start to plays.
With every beat, the roots groove tight,
Turning darkness into pure delight.

Worms and Wonders

Worms slip in their squiggly shoes,
Inviting beetles to share their blues.
"Dig the trenches, let's make a mess!"
Who knew dirt could be such a fest?

With each wiggle, they bring a cheer,
Celebrating soil with lots of beer.
"Raise your shovels, it's time to play!
Let's compost our worries away!"

Forgotten Voices of Fertility

Beneath our feet, a party thrives,
Tiny critters dance, ants in jive.
Worms chuckle at the tales they send,
"Good luck with that!" they wink and bend.

Roots gossip like they're in a café,
"Did you see that bug? He looked so gray!"
Fungi whisper in the friendly dark,
"Let's share some nutrients, now that's a lark!"

The Rhythm of Richness

In the depths, the bass lines thrum,
Grubs and beetles join the drum.
"Good vibes only!" says the grass,
As earthworms wiggle, having a blast.

Moles are headlining the soil show,
While ladybugs sway to and fro.
"Keep it groovy, keep it bright,"
They party hard under the moonlight!

Harmony of the Hidden

Under leaves, the band plays low,
With microbes singing soft and slow.
"Who needs sunlight when we've got flair?"
They share harmonies, filling the air.

Raccoons peek in, "What's the fuss?"
"Just soil shindigs, come join us!"
"Bring your own snacks, we've got the vibe,"
As everyone wobbles, earthworms jive.

Earth's Unraveled Mysteries

Dirt has secrets, oh what a sight,
From worms discussing the best moonlight.
"Is that a root? No, just my sock!"
In the underground, time's a shock!

Mushrooms giggle at the wiggly show,
"Why did the snail move so slow?"
"Because he's packing his house, you see,
And I thought this was a comedy!"

Guardians of the Garden

In the dirt, a party's brewing,
Worms wear capes, with laughter stewing.
Beetles dance to roots' sweet tunes,
While moles debate beneath the moons.

Ladybugs serve tea, quite divine,
Hosting bugs with bottles of wine.
"More compost!" is the evening call,
As earthworms wiggle, having a ball.

The Forgotten Network

Beneath the grass, a web unseen,
Ants gossip 'bout your best kept bean.
"Did you see that? It's an earthworm's bluff!"
"Please, they're not tough, just filled with fluff!"

Mushrooms plot world domination,
While plants hold a secret celebration.
Root neighbors speak in hush-hush tones,
Making plans 'neath their leafy homes.

The Underfoot Chronicles

If you'd peek down, oh what a sight,
Gophers argue, "Who does it right?"
Grass roots giggle as they intertwine,
Shouting, "This patch is surely mine!"

A mole writes tales in dirty prose,
Claiming glory for every rose.
"I dug this hole, where's my parade?"
"Dear friend, you're lost, let's share this shade!"

A Tapestry of Texture

Granules boast of their grainy flair,
"Smoother than silk!" they state with care.
Pebbles nudge, "We're just as grand!"
"Come dance with us, just take a stand!"

A patch of moss holds a fashion show,
Models strut, with a trendy glow.
"Who knew mud could be so chic?"
"Yes!" they all cheer, "Let's merge and peak!"

Narrative of Nutrients

In the garden, peas do prance,
They wiggle in soil, giving nutrients a chance.
Carrots chat with earthworms, so sly,
"Dig deeper!" they shout, as they pass by.

Potatoes play hide and seek in the dirt,
While radishes gossip, their tops in a flirt.
With microbes singing, a catchy refrain,
They summon the sun and dance in the rain.

The Microbial Medley

Tiny critters in a party so grand,
Throwing a bash with grains and sand.
Bacteria bobbing, fungi in a twist,
Making nutrients vanish with a flick of their wrist.

"Who's got the nitrogen?" a voice calls out,
Oh, it's just a molecule, don't scream or shout!
With a fizz and a pop, they mix and collide,
Life underground, where the fun's magnified.

Tales from the Teeming Earth

Once a worm wore a dapper old hat,
Found himself sharing it with a spunky rat.
"You dig, I'll chew!" was their clever decree,
In a world filled with roots, oh what jubilee!

The beetles played jazz, and the fungus swung low,
While a whispering breeze joined in for the show.
Each grain told a story, a twist in each tale,
Underneath the soil, they danced without fail.

Odyssey of the Obscure

In a patch of dirt, where odd things reside,
A gopher wore glasses with worms as his guides.
"Watch out for the shovels!" they'd giggle with glee,
As their world shook and churned, oh, what a spree!

Mole played the flute, and the snail took the stage,
Throwing a bash on a root like a page.
With a crunch and a munch, they all had a blast,
In the cozy dark home where the fun would last.

Ethereal Threads of Earth

Underneath the ground so deep,
Worms are laughing in their sleep.
They squirm and wiggle, what a sight,
Dancing gently through the night.

Tiny parties underground,
With mushrooms spinning all around.
They throw confetti made of spores,
While earthworms boogie on the floors.

Roots that Reach

Roots are stretching, reaching wide,
Tickling bugs who try to hide.
They share gossip with the grass,
Giving secrets a bit of sass.

One root whispered to a tree,
'Did you hear what's new with me?'
'Oh, I've got a bud so bright,
It'll bloom just to cause a fright!'

Nature's Whispers in the Ground

Ants are arguing about the crumbs,
While beetles strut with lots of drums.
'Let's throw a bash,' the faeries cheer,
Underneath the heavens clear.

Mushroom hats and dirtball games,
Everyone's laughing, calling names.
'Hey, I'm the dirt king, can't you see?',
Said the mole with a grin full of glee.

Dance of the Dirt

In the dark, the soil shakes,
As every little creature wakes.
They waltz and twirl, in a muddy spree,
With shovels and rakes, come join me!

Gophers grooving, porcupines sway,
Digging deep, they laugh and play.
'Come and shimmy, roll and slide,',
Said the beetle, with great pride.

Living Layers of History

Beneath our feet, a tale untold,
Layers of stories, some new, some old.
Worms with secrets, ants on quests,
Who knew dirt could be so well-dressed?

With each shovel, a treasure's found,
Old fossils giggle in the ground.
Compost whispers, 'I once was bread,'
Now I'm a feast for roots, well-fed!

Rocks have gossip; they make a scene,
'This pebble here used to be quite keen!'
Time rolls on, and they don't retire,
Just lounge around in the dirt's empire!

The Soil's Embrace

In darkened chambers, life abounds,
Microbes dance on hallowed grounds.
With each scoop, a party starts,
Mushrooms' hats and earthworm arts!

Sometimes soil sings a funny tune,
'Hey there, roots, let's make a moon!'
Cabbages chuckle, and radishes wink,
'Let's plot together, what do you think?'

Pockets of fungi throw wild raves,
'Let's break it down with our spore waves!'
Meanwhile, rocks just relax and roll,
While dirt enjoys its party soul!

Whispers Beneath the Earth

What's that murmur from below?
Is it gossip from plants, who know?
'I'm taller, brighter!' a flower boasts,
While worms just smile, enjoying the toast.

'Got your roots tangled?' a sagebug pleads,
'Well, that's just how love interleaves!'
Beetles giggle, giving high-fives,
In the underworld where chaos thrives.

'Shush now, listen!', a wise old tree,
'Nature's secrets are best set free!'
As minerals mumble, the drama unfolds,
'Can you keep a secret?' the soil beholds!

Tapestry of Tiny Creatures

In the dampness where little ones play,
Each tiny being has something to say.
Ants in tuxedos march on their way,
'Join us for lunch; we serve clay!'

Spider webs sparkled with morning dew,
'We knit our dreams; would you like to view?'
Bees complain, 'Sugar's in the mix!'
But they'll dance to the soil's slick tricks!

Beneath the surface, oh what a ball,
Tiny critters at the earth's grand hall.
Wiggly wigglers and sprightly bugs,
Telling tales of their coffee mugs!

Chorus of the Underground

In the dark, the critters dance,
They wiggle and squirm, given the chance.
A worm wears a top hat, oh what a sight,
Inviting the bugs to a groovy night.

From moles to beetles, the party's alive,
With roots as the guests, they all arrive.
The mushrooms cheer with a cap-tinged grin,
As the fungi groove, let the fun begin!

Rabbits peek in, joining the fun,
Digging through dirt, they're on the run.
Ants are conga-ing, forming a line,
In the muddy club, how they shine!

Oh, to be small in this sprawling ground,
Where laughter and laughter is all around.
With a burp from a gopher, the humor flows,
In the realm below, anything goes!

Network of Nurturers

Underfoot, a web of hatched schemes,
Nurturers smile while plotting their dreams.
Earthworms tweet with a flick of their tails,
Planting funny jokes to sprout in the gales.

Fungi play pranks on roots every day,
With ticklish spores, they giggle and sway.
Mushrooms say, 'Hey! Join in the fray!'
As the roots share tales in a jovial way.

Ants exchange gossip with grace and with flair,
In tiny top hats, they gossip and share.
Each grain of sand holds a giggle so bright,
In the network of life, everything's light!

The soil's a stage where friendships unite,
With earthlings who frolic beneath the night.
For in every inch, there's a party so spry,
In this bustling hum, they all dance and fly!

Odes to Organic Guardians

Oh guardians bustling in the rich, dark soil,
With wriggles and giggles, they happily toil.
Ladybugs laugh as they sprinkle their dew,
While snails do cartwheels, just for the view.

Bees whisper secrets to seedlings nearby,
Tickling petals, all shy and spry.
With a wink and a nod, they organize meets,
For a tea party held 'neath the cabbage seats.

Oh, how the carrots crack jokes from their beds,
Encouraging laughter, pokes at their heads.
Radishes chuckle, 'We're spicier, you know!'
While lettuce just blushes with a sweet, leafy glow.

In this garden realm, a fun brigade thrives,
With giggling roots that lay down their jives.
In this merry pandemonium, out of sight,
Organic custodians boost the delight!

The Enchanted Subsoil

In subsoil lands, where wonders unfold,
Pixies and critters are lively and bold.
With a sprinkle of magic and roots as their dance,
They spin tales of laughter in organic romance.

Gnomes plant puns in the gardens they keep,
With whispers of humor, they never lose sleep.
'Why did the beet get stuck in the mud?'
They chuckle and snicker, 'It thought it was a stud!'

Below every trunk lies a curious quest,
With each little worm trying to jest.
Oh, the tales that the turnips and tubers will share,
Under the laughter, the joy fills the air!

So if you should wander where the soil is deep,
Know that below, the merry ones leap.
In the realm of the roots, the giggles reside,
In enchanted subsoil, let joy be your guide!

Secrets in Every Grain

In tiny bits where worms reside,
They throw a dance, a wiggly slide.
Each grain a tale of muck and mirth,
A laughter riot beneath the earth.

Crickets chirp and moles dig deep,
In hidden realms where secrets sleep.
The beetles boast of their grand feats,
While mushrooms share their funny tweets.

Snails compose their symphony slow,
While microbes gossip, row by row.
Each speck a jester in disguise,
With dirt-packed joy that never dies.

So next time you kneel, bend, and stare,
Remember the giggles lurking there.
In every grain, a joke is spun,
In the soil's heart, there's never a pun.

Beneath the Surface: A World Unseen

Underneath where we can't see,
Quirky critters plot with glee.
They hold wild parties, oh what fun,
With earthworms groovin'—everyone!

Ants with tiny hats parade,
In soil's dance hall, friends are made.
The roots below are quite a crew,
They tickle twigs and twist 'til blue.

Tiny fungi share their charms,
With spores that dance and soil that warms.
And if you listen close, you'll hear,
A raucous laugh, a silly cheer!

So when you dig and find the mess,
Remember all those folks who bless.
The world below—the hidden spree,
Is like a show, just wait and see!

Life Among the Roots

Little roots, they wiggle and writhe,
Throwing shade in a leafy jive.
They weave a tale beneath the sand,
A funny dance, a merry band.

With friends like fungi by their side,
They chase each other, wild and wide.
Earthworms cheer with a squiggly cheer,
As roots perform their grand premiere.

Beneath the grass, so much to see,
A humorous world, oh joy, oh glee!
With every poke, a chuckle comes,
As nature plays her silly drums.

So plant a seed and let it grow,
Join the fun and let it flow.
In earthy depths, it's quite a riot,
Where roots and friends create a diet!

Earth's Lively Labyrinth

In a labyrinth beneath our feet,
Squirrels play hide and seek so neat.
They chewing root snacks, oh what a steal,
While earthworms shake it up for real.

Mice race through tunnels with nifty tricks,
While ants build cities with clever fix.
Each passageway, a comic caper,
In nature's book, a laughable paper.

Beetles strut with a swagger bold,
In this underground world of stories told.
With funny hats and dance routines,
It's quite a scene beneath our greens!

So next time you're out, take a dive,
Explore the maze where antics thrive.
In the cheerful soil, magic spins,
A lively maze where everyone wins.

Guardians of the Garden

In the depths where critters creep,
Worms in jammies, oh so deep.
Napping fungi, they do snore,
While radishes dance on the floor.

Ants hold meetings, what a sight,
Debates on who gets the first bite.
Beetles in ties, so debonair,
Organizing springtime's affair.

Grubs plot mischief, winks abound,
Sneaking snacks from the underground.
Each tiny creature, part of a crew,
Making mischief, who knew?

They whisper secrets, dance and twirl,
In this world where soil meets swirl.
Guardians of greens, they take their post,
In the garden, they're the host.

The Underground Tapestry

Under feet where roots entwine,
Moles wear capes, dressed so fine.
Fungi weave tales, oh so grand,
Spreading stories through the land.

Bacteria sing in bacterial choirs,
While critters spin webs of electric wires.
Earthworms wiggle, plotting a show,
"Let's dance, let's dance!" they gleefully go.

Rocks giggle as they tumble down,
Giving plants coolness, wearing frowns.
"Leave us be," they grumble with flair,
Creating a world that's whimsical wear.

Beneath the surface, life is a play,
A tapestry woven in a crazy way.
In the dark, they laugh and spin,
A secret theatre where the fun begins.

Chronicles of the Dark Earth

Once upon a fungal patch,
A tale of roots began to hatch.
With every scoop, a giggle rose,
As beetles shared their tales in prose.

The worms regaled with earthy tales,
Of muddy journeys and rain-filled gales.
They chuckled hard, without a doubt,
As raindrops fell, they sang out loud.

Invisible heroes, on tiny trips,
Gathering nutrients with little blips.
In their kingdom, laughter flows,
With each squishy step, friendship grows.

Chronicles written without a pen,
Of dirt and mulch, old-timey men.
In caverns dark and damp delight,
They write their history out of sight.

Soil's Subterranean Secrets

Beneath the grass, bugs hold a ball,
With mushrooms tapping, answering the call.
Glowworms twinkle, a disco scene,
As earthworms wiggle in bright green sheen.

Raccoons peek in, judge the dance,
Dirt-covered boots, they take the chance.
"Join us now!" the beetles cry,
As the snails groove by and slyly sigh.

In this realm where giggles bloom,
Snakes slither in, adding to the room.
"Who knew dirt could be so grand?"
They do the conga, hand in hand!

Secrets buried in a jovial wink,
Life below makes us pause and think.
With every layer, surprises galore,
Laughter and fun forever more.

Chronicles of Change Beneath

In the depths where critters play,
Worms throw parties, hip-hip-hooray!
Mice dine on roots, making a mess,
Nature's compost, a tasty fest!

Fungi dance in little shoes,
Sharing secrets, spreading news.
Beetles giggle, ants conspire,
Under the turf, life never tires!

Grubs in pajamas, living the dream,
Dreaming of rivers, a wormy stream.
With tiny top hats, they strut about,
In this party, there's no doubt!

When the rain clouds pour and the mud goes wild,
Earthworms bounce like a cheerful child.
With every squirm, they twist and twirl,
In the great underground, life's a whirl!

Nature's Underground Symphony

Deep in the dirt, where the roots weave,
A symphony plays, best believe!
With bugs as musicians, they take the stage,
Playing their tunes, wise and sage.

Crickets strum on blades of grass,
While cicadas take turns on the pass.
Beatles on drums, and ants in a row,
Creating a show in the soft, rich loam.

The earthworms wiggle, they're quite the sight,
Bouncing to rhythms, feeling just right.
Fungi lead the choir, spread the cheer,
With every note, the underground's clear!

Life is a concert beneath our feet,
With tiny performers, oh so sweet!
When they go quiet, and nature takes pause,
It's just intermission; they're taking a cause!

Life Beneath Layering

Under the layers, oh what a show,
Delightful chaos, all in a row.
Worms in tuxedos, strutting on clay,
While beetles in bowties dance and sway!

Mice in the shadows munching on seeds,
Giggling softly, fulfilling their needs.
Roots intertwine like dancers in pairs,
Beneath the surface, no need for cares!

With glimmers of glop, the mud takes a spin,
Grubs twirl happily, what a win!
The ground is a canvas, let's paint it bright,
With critters and humor, oh what a sight!

Scooping up dirt, we find treasure galore,
Tiny kingdoms hidden, vibrant and more!
Underneath layers of brown and gray,
Lies a rollicking world in infinite play!

Whispered Stories in the Dark

In darkness deep, whispers abound,
Life has stories that can astound.
With critters sharing secrets low,
They giggle and chuckle, keeping it slow.

Worms tell tales of mud-bath romps,
While springtails bounce with little hops.
Fungi listen, taking notes,
Beetles regale, wearing their coats!

Mice trade legends of midnight snacks,
While grubs in pajamas relax on their backs.
A snail tells of an epic quest,
To find the best soil in which to rest!

And as the stories keep rolling in,
The dirt chuckles softly, a hearty grin.
For life underneath, so funny and bold,
Holds whispered moments of laughter untold!

Below the Horizon of Hibernate

Worms in pajamas, dreams of the night,
They wiggle and giggle till morning's first light.
Telling tall tales of roots and of bugs,
A dance party hosted by soil's cuddly thugs.

Under the blanket of dust and delight,
Fungi are knitting by firefly light.
With hats made of leaves and a dance on the ground,
They'll throw a grand ball if the rain comes around.

Microbes narrate their epic of cheer,
Each whispers a secret with a chorus of beer.
While compost confetti falls soft as a dream,
The earth laughs aloud, or so it would seem.

When sleepy roots stretch, oh what a sight,
They twist and they twirl in the moon's gentle light.
Nature's own circus, with giggles and glee,
Who knew beneath ground was such fun to see?

Rhythm of the Rich Realm

Beneath the green carpet, a party does hum,
Moles tap their feet to a bassline of drum.
The beetles are busting a move in a swirl,
While ants bring the snacks, all the best in the world.

A dandelion disco, bright yellow and bold,
Each seed is a dancer, with stories to told.
Life waltzes around, in a vibrant ensemble,
The rhubarb is rapping, and the garlic can fumble.

With each earthy rhythm, the pulses align,
As shovels and rakes join the grand sprawling line.
The tempo keeps growing, an organic delight,
While ladybugs sing sweetly all through the night.

So raise up your glasses, let laughter unfold,
To the soil's rich rhythm, a treasure untold.
For in every small clod, a wild dance persists,
Underfoot magic, oh what could be missed?

Earth's Embrace of Elements

In the depths of the earth, a party does glow,
Where minerals mingle, and thick roots row.
Nitrogen's punchline has everyone hoot,
While phosphorus balances the ultimate loot.

A calcium clown juggles rocks over there,
While water does a waltz, without a care.
Carbon cracks jokes, making everyone laugh,
As microbes spin tales on an old-fashioned raft.

The sand and the silt, they chaotically swirl,
As clay gives a nod, with a sly little twirl.
Together they churn, in a spectacular show,
A grand elemental dance, from below they flow.

So come join the fun in this underground spree,
Where nature's odd cast lives wild and carefree.
In the wiggly world, where we all have a role,
It's a giggle-filled garden, for every soul.

Boundless Beneath Our Feet

Worms in bow ties dance with glee,
Plant roots text you jokes, you see!
A beetle debates with a snail,
While ants plot a glorious trail.

Mice hold meetings, "Who pulled my cheese?"
Caterpillars ponder with great ease.
A dandelion wears a crown so grand,
While fungi cheer from the darkened land.

Beneath the grass, it's quite a show,
With critters playing, putting on a glow.
Tiny parties in the dirt's delight,
Who knew the ground could be so bright?

In every scoop, surprises unfold,
Adventures that never get old.
So next time you walk and don't complain,
Remember the ground has its own funny game!

Earth's Fabled Fabric

Underfoot lies a quirky quilt,
With patches of squishy, muddy silt.
Tangled roots like hair gone wild,
And ladybugs that dance, beguiled.

Gophers giggle as they dig,
Under the moon, they're all pretty big.
A chorus of crickets singing in tune,
While fireflies light it up like noon.

Here the stones gossip, polite and sweet,
As bugs trade secrets on tiny feet.
Dirt's the canvas for nature's jest,
A slapstick world at its very best.

When you step down, remember this cheer,
Life's not just above, it's also down here.
So tip your hat to the dirt and clay,
For they keep the laughter alive every day!

The Lively Web Below

A spider throws a party of threads,
Inviting beetles and all the shreds.
"Don't be shy!" she calls with a wink,
As grasshoppers join in, don't you think?

Moles wear capes, oh what a sight,
Digging tunnels till well past night.
While wormy comedians take the stage,
With punchlines that make the beetles rage.

Ants serve snacks made of fallen crumbs,
"More for you, and more for mums!"
In this vibrant world where the funny throngs,
Who knew the muck could hold such songs?

So when you tread, remember each cheer,
The underworld's jest is loud and clear.
Join the giggles from below your feet,
And tap dance with the soil—that's quite a feat!

Time and Texture Underfoot

Rocks play cards, "Who bets a grain?"
While moss takes bets like it's all just a game.
The trees root for the player's fun,
As squirrels giggle, "Oh, we've won!"

A toad croaks jokes in a funky tone,
While ladybugs whistle, "Next prize is home!"
The grass hums softly, in rhythm and rhyme,
Each layer of earth knows it's party time.

Compost heaps swap the wildest tales,
Of distant travels on leafy trails.
In this merry mash of shadow and light,
It's a carnival, hidden but bright.

So next time you stroll, let's hear a shout,
For the laughter beneath—no doubt a rout!
With every step, feel the vibrant beat,
Life's a circus down there, oh what a treat!

The Soil's Silent Conversations

In darkness, worms whisper low,
To roots, they pass on info-flow.
A beetle laughs, a slug takes notes,
While ants all wear their tiny coats.

Beneath the surface, fungi sway,
Sharing gossip, come what may.
"Hey, did you hear about the tree?"
"The one that danced with bumblebee?"

Earthcrust grins, and stones confide,
They joke about the rainy tide.
With every drop, a party starts,
As mud winks back, it steals our hearts.

So if you kneel, just lend an ear,
You'll find a world that's full of cheer.
For every sprinkle and every clod,
There's laughter shared in this soggy pod.

Microcosms of Mud

In every puddle, life runs wild,
A tadpole croaks, a worm's a child.
A snail slides past with practiced grace,
While mudbugs keep a poker face.

The little critters play their games,
A dance-off under all the flames.
"Who can jump the highest?" they shout,
While raindrops cheer and twist about.

A spider spins a silky web,
Counting all the bugs she'd ebb.
"First one to catch a fly will win!"
The drama unfolds in the muddy din.

In this tiny world, there's much to do,
A party hidden from our view.
So next time you step in some gloopy mud,
Just smile at the life in the squelchy flood.

Dances of Decay

Down in the compost, hearts beat loud,
As fungi sway, they're feeling proud.
The leaves all chuckle, turning brown,
While critters boogie in their gown.

Rotting fruit throws a wild party,
With microbes grooving, oh so hearty.
"More bananas here," says the rat,
As old apple cores bathe in chat.

Gasses bubble, the stench is sweet,
Yet all the dancers find their beat.
The cycle spins, with twirls and leaps,
While nature grins, and silence weeps.

So next time you toss out some scraps,
Think of the dance with all its laps.
For even decay has its own spree,
A cheeky conga under the tree.

The Poetry of Particles

In tiny worlds, the bits do rhyme,
As atoms gossip all the time.
A carbon quip, a nitrogen jest,
These particles know what's for the best.

"Hey, did you see that sunny day?
All the plants have come out to play!"
Said silicon to dirt and clay,
"Let's throw a party in this bay!"

The minerals dance in perfect sync,
While water's splash gets them to think.
A symphony of lively tunes,
Where every grain sparkles and croons.

So dive right down, and take a look,
A tale of joy in every nook.
For in the layers, there's much to see,
As nature writes its own decree.

Threads of Fertility

Worms wear tuxedos, munching leaves,
Dancing 'neath the surface, like teenage thieves.
They wiggle and giggle, so full of zest,
Turning trash to treasure, oh what a quest!

The microbes throw parties, it's quite the scene,
Feasting on roots, making soil pristine.
They surely know how to throw a good bash,
Transforming the leftovers with a little dash.

And ants form a line, like a caravan rare,
Marching in rhythm with a crumb to share.
"Excuse me," they say, "but we're on a roll,
Building our empire, feel the control!"

So here's to the life that rolls on down there,
With critters and chaos beyond compare.
They'll tell you a tale, if you care to listen,
Of gardening shindigs where the greens all glisten.

Secrets of the Subsoil

Down in the depths where the sunlight fades,
Worms write their memoirs with tiny spades.
They dig deep secrets, never make a sound,
In a world of wonder, a treasure is found.

Fungi wear crowns, twisting through the gloom,
They're bringing the party—the underground boom!
All with a mushroom hat, so dapper and spry,
In the vast hidden ballroom where critters fly by.

The grubs throw a rager, they rumble and play,
With laughter that bubbles up through the clay.
"Who invited the beetles?" a wise old snail said,
"They're dancing so wild, I'm wishing them dead!"

In this kingdom below, life's a mischievous game,
Where even the roots have a wild, wacky name.
So tiptoe along, respect what's in sight,
In the depths of the earth, every bug stays tight!

Beneath the Bark: Earth's Pulse

Under the bark, where the beetles reside,
Things get a little quirky, let's take a ride.
They laugh at the trees, saying, "Look at us go!
We're dancing with fungi, in rhythms we flow!"

With squirrels at the helm, a nutty parade,
They're stashing their snacks in a high-octane spade.
"Hey, pass the acorn!" a chipmunk would squeak,
As they plot for dominance, oh what a week!

Earthworms are grooving, slick with ambition,
They worm their way up, it's a grand expedition.
"Hey roots, watch your back, we're on the attack,
We're turning this soil into our very own snack!"

Under the bark, life's a vibrant affair,
With each little critter showing flair and flair.
So next time you dig, remember the fun,
For beneath the ground, the party's never done!

The Artisans of Organic

Crafty little critters, the artisans gleam,
Turning the mundane into a compost dream.
With a shovel and laughter, they mix and they churn,
In the art of decay, there's so much to learn.

The beetles are sculptors, chiseling fine,
Creating a landscape where everything's divine.
"From scraps to fertilizer, we're quite the crew,
Watch and you'll see what a little love can do!"

The ants are like butlers, serving the bees,
With crumbs of delight found under the trees.
"Please, hold the nectar; we're in the zone,
This buffet of pollen is all on loan!"

So here's to the artisans, clever and spry,
In the theater of dirt, they reach for the sky.
With a wink and a wiggle, they keep us in thrall,
In the realm of the organic, they dazzle us all!

Echoes of the Earth

Underneath the ground, they dance and prance,
Worms in a conga, a squirmy romance.
Fungi wear hats, all spongy and bright,
Throwing a party in the dead of night.

Ants serve up tea with a side of dirt,
While roots gossip softly, with no hint of hurt.
Beetles in bow ties roll out the cheese,
And moles break the ice with a joke or a wheeze.

While beetroot debates with a bold radish,
The carrots lounge back, feeling quite lavish.
It's a banquet of laughs down below the green,
Where everyone's welcome, and no one's a queen.

So if you should dig and find this glee,
Remember, dear friend, keep it a mystery!
The garden is bustling, it's quite the affair,
Just watch your step, there's laughter in the air!

The Soil's Secret Conversations

In the dark and the damp, life swirls all around,
With earthworms composing their own silly sound.
'Hey rock, do you mind if I wiggle right here?'
'Not at all,' the stone chuckles, 'let's share a cold beer!'

The mushrooms are gossiping, tipsy on rain,
Discussing the rumors of that pesky young grain.
A dandelion's teasing a stubborn old sprout,
'You wish you were leafy, now's that not a clout?'

Every root has a tale about what it has seen,
From floods to the creatures, both humble and mean.
With whispers so funny, they tickle the dirt,
From fables of beetles to tales of their hurt.

So listen quite closely, amidst all the fun,
For conversations in soil have only begun!
With laughter and wonder, the secrets unwind,
In the grand underground where you rarely will find.

Murmurs of Microbes

Beneath our two feet, a party unfolds,
With microbes and bacteria, the mischief they hold.
Tiny jesters with gowns made of fluff,
Throwing confetti of fungi and stuff.

'Hey, how's it going? Did you catch the last show?'
A student of soil sitting next to a crow.
'Best performance yet! Left me rolling with glee!'
'I heard the worms cry, it was a sight to see!'

With laughter so soft, the nutrients blend,
While roots high-five as they wiggle and send.
A comedy club under raisin-like skies,
Where even the rocks can't help but rise.

So peek underneath, if you dare to explore,
These micro-mischief-makers are never a bore.
With giggles and wiggles, they dazzle the night,
A humorous world that's out of our sight!

The Veiled Vibrancy

In shadows and roots where the party's a mix,
Life's unraveling secrets, with laughs and kicks.
Nematodes waltz, they've got rhythm untold,
While the grasses throw shade, feeling mighty bold.

With glee in their hearts, they spin round and round,
Tiny creatures jiving, all under the ground.
'Hey clover,' they shout, 'join the groove, don't be shy!'
The daisies roll over, while giving a sigh.

Amidst all this bustle, a caterpillar sways,
To the tune of the roots in a funky ballet.
The soil's a stage, not a place to fret,
For every small beetle is a ballerina's pet.

So dig just a little, and let laughter rise,
To see all the craziness cloaked in disguise.
It's a vibrant circus beneath our sole weight,
Where the joy of the ground turns mundane into great!

Earth's Hidden Alchemy

In the dark, where the critters play,
The microbes dance in their own ballet.
Mixing up clay with a wink and a nod,
Creating a party for the hungry sod.

Worms in tuxedos, earth's little chefs,
Whipping up compost, no need for the rest.
Turning scraps into gold, or so they claim,
While the plants below whisper, 'We'll share the fame!'

Nutrients party, dressed up so bright,
They slide through the roots like they're out for a night.
With a bubble and squeak, in the soil they wade,
Making sure that the veggies get perfectly made.

Beneath our feet, there's a ruckus and roar,
Where fungi and bacteria conduct their lore.
Nature's pranksters, they tickle the ground,
And leave us to wonder what else can be found.

Life's Quilt Below Ground

Underfoot lies a patchwork divine,
Woven with roots like a grand design.
Each thread tells a tale, so silly and strange,
Of beetles in bowties and insects in range.

Dirt's the fabric, it's cozy and warm,
Where life's little critters cheerfully swarm.
They stitch together bugs, mold, and a slug,
Creating a quilt that would give you a hug.

The gophers are tailors with scissors and care,
Building their dwellings with a fashionable flair.
While ants and their buddies play hide and seek,
In this underground shop where the laughter's unique.

With a pat and a poke, let's dig in the fun,
Discovering treasures where the rascals run.
Oh, what a party that thrives in the earth,
A quirky collection of life and of mirth.

Murmurs of Molecules

Tiny whispers in the soil tonight,
Molecules giggle, it's quite a delight.
They huddle together, gossiping so low,
Sharing secrets of rain and the sun's golden glow.

Carbon and nitrogen swap silly romance,
While oxygen twirls in a froggy-like dance.
Hydrogen chuckles, puffing out steam,
As photosynthesis dreams up a gleam!

Hydrolysis bakes mud pies in glee,
While the fungi are chanting, 'Let's brew a spree!'
With a twist and a turn, they mix it all round,
As the roots stomp their feet to the underground sound.

Oh, what a hullabaloo beneath our bare feet,
Where molecules mingle and frolic to beat!
Join in the chatter, let's not pass it by,
Life's tiny jesters, oh my, oh my!

The Lifenurturer Underfoot

Buried treasures in my backyard roam,
Critters make music, call it their home.
Bacteria boast, 'We're kings of the clay!'
While worms spin tales of their gooey buffet.

Moles with their shovels dig tunnels of charm,
While roots hold hands, never causing harm.
The great underground orchestra starts to play,
As the earthworms wiggle, leading the fray.

Fungi bring cupcakes with sprinkles on top,
While beetles break dance, not wanting to stop.
The soil's a carnival, laughter's the sound,
And the drumming of raindrops brings everyone 'round.

So take off your shoes and join in the fun,
This life underground never comes undone.
With a sprinkle of humor and a dash of delight,
We celebrate earth's party every night!

Symphony of Subterranean Life

In the dark where worms wiggly play,
They hold concerts at the end of the day.
Beetles on trumpets, ants in a choir,
Compose a tune that never tires.

Moles dance around in a wild ballet,
While roots tap on beats, hip-hip-hooray!
The fungi sing harmonies so sweet,
They groove underground to nature's beat.

Tiny critters are truly the stars,
Growing their fame beneath rocks and jars.
With soil as their stage, they boogie all night,
In this earthy club, their future is bright.

Who knew that beneath our feet so low,
Life's a party with plants in tow?
From muck and mud, joy takes its toll,
This ground is alive—let's rock 'n' roll!

The Hidden Heart of the Ground

Down where the sun rarely shines through,
There's a hidden realm that's funny and new.
Gophers gossip, their secrets to share,
About humans above who think they're so rare.

With dirt as their duvet, they plot and conspire,
To tickle the roots as their mischief grows higher.
Potato jokes abound, they're a-peeling,
While carrots are laughing—they're great at concealing.

Under rocks, they hold every debate,
About the best nutrients that they can create.
They giggle and squirm, the bugs have a ball,
In the warmth of the earth, they just cannot stall!

Life's a riot beneath the ground's crust,
With every little critter filled with great lust.
They thrive in their home, so cozy and round,
Unveiling the humor in the hidden ground!

Veins of Vitality

In the veins of the earth, there's a party unseen,
Where microbes complain about life being routine.
"Oy, another day in this stubborn old mud,"
Cried a grumpy old worm while he tunneled for crud.

Roots are the highways of veggie delight,
While fungi keep bustling from morning 'til night.
"We're the real stars!" they declare with a grin,
As grass plants nod softly and join in the din.

With nutrients flowing like grape jelly spread,
They tell wild tales of their wisdom so red.
"Oh to be human!" a young sprout would sigh,
"If they only knew how much fun it is to fly!"

So beneath our feet, a tale's interlaced,
Where laughter erupts in this wonderful space.
A kingdom of quirks, of yucks and of fun,
In the veins that connect us, when all said and done!

Dance of the Decomposers

What's that jig happening down in the muck?
Oh, it's just maggots—having some luck!
With scraps and with leftovers, they party on,
Creating new life—'tis the circle's song.

"Hey, check out that leaf!" a young beetle cries,
"Let's have a feast 'til the sun starts to rise!"
While bugs do the worm, and spores take a twirl,
In this merry affair, as joy starts to unfurl.

The dancers all shimmy in rich, tasty blends,
Transforming the soil for the plants and their friends.
With guffaws and goose steps, they carry on well,
Giving life to the earth—more stories to tell!

So, when you look down, down deep in the dirt,
Know there's laughter and mischief and never a hurt.
The decomposers delight in a bouncing parade,
Making fun out of what seems a grand charade!

Whispers Beneath Our Feet

Little critters dance with glee,
Microbe parties, wild and free.
Worms in bow ties, sipping tea,
Underneath, the fun's a spree!

Ants wear hats and strut in line,
Fungi sing, their voices fine.
Earthworms boast of great design,
A crazy world that's simply divine!

Rocks debate in mellow tones,
Tiny stones with silly bones.
Roots gossip like old-time phones,
Telling tales in hidden zones.

So if you stomp, just stop, my friend,
Listen close, and soon you'll blend.
In this soil, the fun won't end,
Join the jokes; your heart will mend!

The Hidden Symphony Underground

A chorus hums beneath the ground,
With roots and rocks in leaps and bounds.
Mice play flutes, making joyful sound,
While worms tap dance; it's quite profound!

Mycelium string quartets play,
Singing softly night and day.
Worms do the cha-cha, hip-hip hooray,
A soil concert, come what may!

Grubs are drummers, making noise,
Earth's little band of merry boys.
Beneath the dirt, they share their joys,
Creating music, oh what ploys!

So pull off your shoes and take a seat,
Join the fun and find the beat.
In every clump, there's humor sweet,
So stay awhile, don't feel the heat!

Earth's Quiet Architects

Tiny builders, oh so sly,
Constructing homes where secrets lie.
Moles with hard hats, what a sight,
Building tunnels, oh what delight!

Raccoons supervise the way,
Planning picnics by the bay.
With each shovel and scoot, they sway,
Digging jokes in the light of day!

Each pebble tells a story sweet,
Of grand designs beneath our feet.
With laughter echoing in their beat,
They shape the ground, a light-hearted feat!

So when you tread, remember this,
There's more than dirt, there's joy and bliss.
A bustling world you cannot miss,
Underneath the ground's warm kiss!

Beneath the Surface: A Soil Tale

Once upon a time in dirt so grand,
A party brewed in every strand.
Caterpillars played in a merry band,
While tall grass served the snacks on hand!

Worms told tales of their last spree,
With radishes chuckling, oh what glee!
The soil was alive, can't you see?
In this party, everyone's free!

Ladybugs rolled in laughter loud,
Rooted friends formed a happy crowd.
With tiny top hats, they felt so proud,
Their antics made the earth feel bowed.

So dive down, don't you fear a fall,
Join in the fun; there's room for all.
In the soil's embrace, heed the call,
Where every critter has a ball!

Life's Layers

Beneath our feet, a party's brewing,
Worms in tuxedos, so amusing!
They sip on dew and dance around,
In this rich world that's underground.

Roots are mingling, oh what a sight,
Waving to bugs, all feeling just right.
They trade their secrets, giggles abound,
In this top soil joy that knows no bounds.

Hidden and Deep

Moles throw shindigs, no invites sent,
Rats are the servers, all really bent!
Ants in tuxes march in success,
Squirrels bring snacks—a furry finesse.

The mushrooms have wisdom, they drop sage advice,
"Don't play too deep, or you'll roll the dice!"
The crickets laugh at the underground spree,
While beetles rock out, as wild as can be.

The Unseen Kaleidoscope

In this fertile realm, things twist and twirl,
Nematodes do the tango, what a whirl!
Fungi are decorators, draping the room,
While creepy-crawlers bring life to the gloom.

The colors of life's tiniest crew,
Are bright and vibrant, what a view!
Taproot DJs spin, the bass shaking ground,
In this lively hideaway, joy is abound.

Earth's Busy Bureaucracy

Buzzing with deals, a fungus decree,
Earthworms are lobbyists, clever as can be.
With minerals traded and moisture tallied,
The micromanager ants, all slightly rallied!

Excavators on breaks, the soil committee,
Resolves their disputes with a wiggly bitty.
"Let's work together, for richer delight!"
In paperwork mess, they party at night.

The Subtle Science Beneath

With dirt so rich, there's magic in play,
Microbes have meetings to plot out the day.
"Hey, let's giggle at the gardener's toil!"
As they munch on squished roots deep in the soil.

Wiggly strategies, and tactical plot,
The sand grains giggle, "We've got a lot!"
Unseen connections build cities so fine,
And all underfoot—what a sneaky design!

Stardust in the Dark

In the midnight garden, worms all grin,
They wiggle and giggle, as they begin.
A mushroom speaks up, quite tall and proud,
"I'm the best fun guy!" says he to the crowd.

Roots high-five each other, down in their place,
Wiggly dance moves in this earthy space.
"No shoes required, just bring your own dirt!"
They shout with glee, covered in shirt and skirt.

Rabbits hopping by, they join in the cheer,
With carrots as microphones, they all persevere.
"Let's throw a party, the grass is our floor!"
With popcorn packed soil, who could ask for more?

So under the stars, while the critters convene,
The soil is alive, a true little scene.
With laughter and joy, they twirl in delight,
In this quirky world, everything feels right.

Beneath the Canopy: Life Interwoven

Deep in the shadows where no one can peek,
The ants throw a party and dance 'til the week.
With tiny top hats, and mayflies in sync,
They tiptoe on roots, getting close to the brink.

A beetle plays chess with a lazy old snail,
While spiders weave tales on a silky trail.
"Checkmate!" shouts Beetle, all covered in glee,
As Snail just replies, "That's fine, it's just me!"

Tree frogs serenade with ribbits so loud,
While the woodpeckers tap, like a drummer unbowed.
"Join us!" they plead, "in the soil's warm embrace,
We're all here together, let's party, let's race!"

The roots intertwine like the best of friends,
Spreading good humor, as laughter transcends.
In this leafy world, with a wink and a grin,
The best hidden wonders, where adventure begins.

In the Embrace of the Earth

Under the surface, where the wild things play,
The gophers spin tales in their cheeky way.
"I dug really deep, found a treasure to keep!"
Said the chipmunk with pride, now, let's take a leap!

Dirt clouds above as they hop to the beat,
Earthworms pop out for a wiggly greet.
"Can you dance on your tail? How about on a root?"
While bluebirds laugh loudly, it's all quite a hoot!

A squirrel shows off with a twirling grand move,
With acorns for drums, he's got something to prove.
While crickets compose their own jazzy line,
In this underground theater, they shine and they shine.

So come take a dive, give your shoes a rest,
In the cozy soil world, we all feel our best.
Amidst all this chaos, pure joy finds its girth,
In the giggly deep layers, the heart of the Earth.

Roots of the Unsung

Beneath the broad leaves, where few dare to roam,
A chorus of fungi declare, "This is home!"
"Let's throw puns and jokes, plant a laugh or two,"
With claps from the thistles, they all shout, "Woohoo!"

Tiny elks inching forth with a slow little trot,
Whispering secrets that they just cannot spot.
"I saw a big squirrel wearing shades 'n a coat!"
The gossip erupts, like waves on a boat.

Grasshoppers hop high to the tune of the breeze,
With an air of cool, they do it with ease.
"Can you believe it? The roots got a laugh,
They tickled the daisies! Oh, what a gaffe!"

So under the soil, where laughter is spun,
The life we don't see is still full of fun.
In this hidden realm, where the giggles prevail,
Let's drink to the roots and the beats of the trail!

Microbial Melodies

Tiny critters sing and chirp,
In a soil-made concert, they often burp.
Worms do the tango, it's quite a sight,
While beetles groove, oh, what a night!

Fungi flaunt their thread-like shoes,
Debating if they should dance or snooze.
Bacteria start a pop band, oh dear,
Their harmonies—slightly grim, yet clear!

A nematode joins, with moves so bold,
Telling tales of treasures yet untold.
Grains tap their toes beneath the ground,
In this wet wonderland, vibes abound!

So next time you dig, don't just grumble,
Listen close, let your heart rumble.
For beneath your feet, a show is on,
In the soil realm, life's never gone!

The Dark Dance of Nutrients

In the shadows, calcium winks,
While magnesium saunters, or so it thinks.
Potassium prances, vibrant and spry,
Trading rumors with phosphorus nearby.

Sulfur's got moves, it twists with flair,
While nitrogen giggles, fluffing its hair.
Together they sway, a nutrient ball,
Mixing and mingling, they're having a ball!

Organic matter shows off its charms,
With compost confetti, it means no harms.
They twirl and they'll whirl, whisper and tease,
Playing hide-and-seek like a bunch of bees!

So when you plant, hear the beat of the ground,
In this nutrient dance, life can be found.
Not just dirt, but a party so fine,
Below your feet, it's a chance to shine!

Soil's Silent Symphony

In muted tones, the earth does play,
With rustling roots in a dance ballet.
Compost crinkles, a hushed applause,
As nature's orchestra finds its cause.

Beetles click-clack, a drumbeat delight,
While ants form a chorus, perfect and tight.
Fungi whisper sweet notes to the air,
In a silent symphony, no one's aware.

Earthworms thump like bass guitars,
Twisting tunes beneath the stars.
Microbes hum in a rhythmic grind,
Creating music only they can find!

So dig your dreams, hear the song of the land,
In this soil symphony, life's never bland.
For every scoop might hold a surprise,
A concert awaits under open skies!

Beneath the Canopy: A Hidden Realm

Under the trees, a secret scene,
Where roots spread gossip, and fungi convene.
The cool earth chuckles, a quiet friend,
As critters plan their wiggles and bends.

Bugs trade stories of tasty roots,
While mushrooms giggle in fancy suits.
They throw a party, with snacks galore,
Dirt cake, anyone? Who could ask for more?

Gophers in tuxedos, quite the sight,
Jiving with moles 'til the morning light.
The whispers of life flow through the ground,
In this hidden realm, joy can be found!

So when you walk on the forest floor,
Remember the antics behind the door.
For beneath the canopy, laughter reigns,
In a quirky world where no one complains!

www.ingramcontent.com/pod-product-compliance
Lightning Source LLC
Chambersburg PA
CBHW070322120526
44590CB00017B/2788